THE
Archive Photographs
SERIES

BRIGHTON
AND
HOVE

GREETINGS CARD. Posted in Brighton in August 1908, this card had written on the back the terse message, 'Having a very nice time'. This was typical of the cards produced by postcard makers at this time, with the name of the resort and the inset picture changed as necessary. The photograph of the aquarium was evidently considered to be typical of the delights offered by Brighton at this time.

THE
Archive Photographs
SERIES

BRIGHTON
AND
HOVE

Compiled by
Tony Wales

CHALFORD

First published 1997
Copyright © Tony Wales, 1997

The Chalford Publishing Company
St Mary's Mill, Chalford,
Stroud, Gloucestershire, GL6 8NX

ISBN 0 7524 0755 4

Typesetting and origination by
The Chalford Publishing Company
Printed in Great Britain by
Redwood Books, Trowbridge

*For my Granddaughters
Heather and Emma*

Contents

BRIGHTON BEACH, BOATS AND BATHING HUTS. A pleasantly busy picture from 1902, although the beach appears less crowded than on many other pictures from this period. The bathing huts with their large wheels were still in fashion at this time, although coming to the end of their long lives. Note also the black umbrellas used as sunshades, and the seats for which a charge was made. Hats were almost obligatory - even the gent who is paddling has kept his bowler on.

The Pavilion, Brighton

BRIGHTON PAVILION. This picture from early this century epitomises the fashionable face of the town, as ladies and gentlemen stroll in the sunshine.

Introduction

My love affair with Brighton began a long time ago, back in the 1920s. It was then that my parents and my aunt took me on day trips to 'The Queen of the South' (to use just one of the many names bestowed on the town through the years). During this period of my life, I also had a close attachment to Littlehampton, and was familiar with all its nooks and crannies. My grandparents lived there, and so it was almost my second home. In fact, familiarity meant that although I thoroughly enjoyed all it had to offer, I tended to take it for granted as part of my normal childhood.

But Brighton was different. Firstly, because I saw it by means of single day visits, and I was therefore very conscious that there was a lot more to it than I could absorb in a few hours. Secondly, it was certainly a more lively place than either my own small home town, or cosy Littlehampton. At that time I had not experienced any other large towns, not even London, so 'London by the Sea', with its two piers, aquarium, electric railway and so much more, seemed the epitome of all that spelt excitement for a small boy.

Later my appreciation sharpened as I grew to appreciate Brighton's amazing wealth of history and cast of characters. It would be pointless to reiterate even a small part of all this in my introduction. In any case, it has been done so comprehensively by many fine writers (witness the brief bibliography on page 8).

I have tried to avoid the too familiar pictures, or those already shown in books currently in print. Readers who know my previous work, will not be surprised to note that I have concentrated very much on social history and folklore of the Brighton area, of which there is an embarrassment of riches. Of course the photographs really tell the story; but I hope that my words supplement rather than merely accompany the pictures.

Acknowledgements

This book could not have been compiled without all the tremendous help I have had from others, both with the loan of pictures and with information. I must therefore record my great debt to all of the following.

Mr A. Bissell, Mrs L. Canham, Mr J. Cannon, Mr C.W. Cramp, Miss M. Curtis, Miss H. Daly, Miss V. Downer, the *Evening Argus* (for pictures from the *Brighton Herald*), Mr B. Evershed, Mr S. Goddard, Mr M. Hayes and Mr R. Knibb of the West Sussex County Library Service, Mr R. Merrifield, Mr J. Muggeridge, Mr and Mrs J. Payne, Mr C. Phillips, Mr J.R. Thomas, Mr I. Wale, Mr T. Wilcox (Curator of Hove Museum and Art Gallery), Mrs M.C. Willis.

Some of these people are no longer with us, but I hope the inclusion of their names will serve as a tiny tribute to their memory. I must also record my debt to the many postcard shops and dealers from whom I have bought picture postcards and photographs during the past forty or so years. Also a special thank you to Mr David Turner who copied many of the old photographs so expertly. If I have left anyone out, or if I have inadvertently trespassed on anyone's copyright, may I tender my apologies. A word about dating: it is often difficult to decide on the precise date for a photograph when few details are available. Please forgive me if I have got this wrong, and feel free to correct me if you feel you know better.

Tony Wales has written widely on Sussex, and his books include: *We Wunt be Druve* (1976), *A Sussex Garland* (1979), *The West Sussex Village Book* (1984), *Sussex Customs, Curiosities and Country Lore* (1990), *Sussex Ghosts and Legends* (1992), *The Landscapes of West Sussex* (1994).

Bibliography

Ainsworth, Harrison: *Ovingdean Grange*
Aitcheson, George: *Unknown Brighton*. 1926
Betjeman, John and Gray, J.S.: *Victorian and Edwardian Brighton*. 1972
Blaker, Nathaniel Paine: *Sussex in Bygone Days*. 1919
Candlin, Lillian: *Memories of Old Sussex*. 1987
Carder, Timothy: *The Encyclopedia of Brighton*. 1990
Dale, Anthony: *Fashionable Brighton*. 1947
Dale, Antony: *Brighton Town and Brighton People*. 1976
Dale, Antony: *Brighton Churches*. 1989
Elleray, D.R.: *Brighton - A Pictorial History*. 1987
Flower, Raymond: *The Old Ship*. 1986
Gilbert, Edmund, M.: *Brighton Between the Wars*. 1976
Harrison, Frederick and North, James Sharp: *Old Brighton, Old Hove, Old Preston*. 1937.
Hayden, Roger: *West Blatchington Windmill and Village*. 1993.
Middleton, Judy: *A History of Hove*. 1979.
Moens, S.M.: *Rottingdean, the Story of a Village*. 1952.
Musgrave, Clifford: *Life in Brighton*. 1970.
Nairn, Ian and Pevsner, Nikolaus: *The Buildings of England*. 1965
Noakes, Daisy: *The Town Beehive*.
Ogley, B., Currie, I., and Davison, M.: *The Sussex Weather Book*. 1991
Paul, Albert: *Poverty, Hardship but Happiness*. 1974
Powell, Margaret: *Below Stairs*. 1968
Ryman, Ernest: *The Romance of the Old Chain Pier*. 1996
Sitwell, Osbert and Barton, Margaret: *Brighton*. 1935
Many guides, maps, magazines and newspapers.

One

Beach and Town

THE CHAIN PIER, c. 1890s. Arguably the loveliest of England's seaside piers, Brighton chain pier was completed in 1823 at a cost of £30,000. It had a relatively short life, succumbing to its constant enemies, the wind and the waves, in 1896. Admission to the pier cost two pence – quite a lot at the time. A song current at the time expressed the locals' feelings in this manner:

> *But of all the sweet pleasures that Brighton can boast;*
> *A walk on the chain pier delighted me most,*
> *That elegant structure, light, airy and free,*
> *Like the work of enchantment, hangs over the sea.*

THE CHAIN PIER. An earlier and very atmospheric picture with a definite air of loneliness. One of my treasured possessions is a copy of a tape recording made by an old Brighton lady in 1969, when she was 84. Her father was late home one evening, and she had gone out to meet him. She then tells how she heard a most tremendous crash, and when her father reached her he said, 'Do you know the chain pier has gone'. Another observer watched as the structure disappeared into the waves, a solitary light remaining until the last moment. A few things have survived: two small toll-houses were removed and eventually used on the Palace Pier, and a sundial has ended up in Balcombe churchyard.

West Pier, Brighton

THE WEST PIER. Built in 1863/6, the photograph shows the pier early this century. It cost £27,000 and was one of the first seaside piers built mainly for pleasure purposes. At the opening, one speaker said that he hoped the ladies would patronise it, 'For where the ladies were gathered, the gentlemen would be sure to congregate also'. We don't know now whether the ladies approved or not, but the attractions included such delights as performing fleas and a cannon which was fired daily at noon.

THE WEST PIER BY NIGHT. From the same period as the last picture, this was a sight beloved by Brighton visitors. The very elegant and attractive pier was designed by that doyen of pier engineers, Eugenius Birch (1818-84), who also built Blackpool's North Pier. Eventually it was allowed to fall into ruin and the Southern end of the pier closed in 1970; complete closure followed five years later. Since then tremendous efforts have been made to rebuild and reopen it.

The Palace Pier & New Winter Gardens Brighton

THE PALACE PIER, *c.* 1920. This was intended as a replacement for the old chain pier. After many delays, it opened on 20 May 1899. The initial phase cost £137,000, and the pier was completed with the opening of a landing stage and pavilion on 9 April 1901. In 1930 a new entrance was made and the clock tower erected. It was extended in 1938 when a 'Big Wheel' was added to the pier head, although this did not meet with everyone's approval.

THE PALACE PIER BY NIGHT, *c.* 1912. Acknowledged to be the finest pleasure pier ever built, this picture with its watery reflections certainly underlines this claim. But things were not always so happy: the pier was damaged in the Second World War and a gap was cut in the middle. It was reopened in 1946, but in October 1973 a 70 ton barge damaged the structure and the theatre partly collapsed. In 1984 many fresh attractions were added and the pier continues to go from strength to strength.

MIXED BATHING

BATHING MACHINE. A picture from early this century, when such contrivances were perhaps becoming a little dated, as huts of this sort had been giving sterling service on Brighton beach since the eighteenth century. A guide book of 1794 explains how they were used: 'By means of a hook-ladder the bather ascends the machine, which is formed of wood and raised on high wheels. He is drawn to a proper distance from the shore, and then plunges into the sea; guides attending on each side to assist him. The guides are strong, active and careful; and in every respect, adapted to their employment.' The guides mentioned were probably known as Dippers, the two most famous of whom were Martha Gunn and Smoaker Miles. A Brighton rhyme immortalised them thus:

> There's plenty of dippers and jokers,
> And salt-water rigs for your fun.
> The King of them all is 'Old Smoaker',
> The Queen of them 'Old Martha Gunn.'
> The ladies walk out in the morn,
> To taste of the salt-water breeze,
> They ask if the water is warm,
> Says Martha, 'Yes, Ma'am, if you please.'

PADDLERS BENEATH THE PALACE PIER. In this photograph, taken around the turn of the century, there is a lovely contrast between the young girls in their white outfits and the elderly ladies in black with their umbrellas. Attractions come and go, but the enjoyment offered by the sand and the sea is timeless. In the early nineteenth century, the Brighton town crier announced that a Holland smock, a pair of silk stockings, and a gold ring, were to be offered as prizes for a race run by ladies on the beach. A big crowd assembled at the appointed time, only to find later that the whole thing was a hoax.

BRIGHTON BEACH. This picture was taken during the halycon days before the First World War. There are quite a few empty seats, possibly because they cost a penny. Anyway, pebbles make a good substitute. Note the Edwardian Nanny type figure in black, standing over her charge. Brighton pebbles were avidly collected by children at this time – a shop in Pool Valley even published a booklet giving the names of different types of pebbles found on Brighton Beach, including Jaspers, Choanites, Eylchonites and Crystals.

Brighton Beach.

ARMY HORSES ENJOYING THE SEA. The picture is undated, but the time is probably around that of the First World War. Brighton has a long history of connections with the military. The song and dance tune known as Brighton Camp, goes back to at least the eighteenth century. The best known words of the song (*The Girl I Left Behind Me*) tell of the feelings of a soldier sent to serve at Brighton Camp, who is longing for the girl back home. There are, of course, many different versions of this song, and it also makes a very fine dance reel.

FEEDING THE PIGEONS ON THE WEST PIER. Although pigeons are classed as pests, visitors always love feeding them. This undated photograph is probably from the 1920s or '30s, when roving photographers snapped unsuspecting holidaymakers, handing them a slip of paper to take to Happy Snaps in exchange for copies of their pictures (for a payment, of course). This was all part of a good day out at the seaside.

THE AQUARIUM, early 1900s. This photograph shows the ornate clock tower over the entrance, before it was removed when the aquarium was rebuilt in 1929. The aquarium was the idea of Eugenius Birch, the famous engineer of the West Pier. The project was completed in 1872, costing £130,000, and formally opened in August of that year. The central hall housed a 100 ft tank holding 110,000 gallons of water. There was also a reading room, restaurant, fernery, and later a cinema (known as the Aquarium Kinema).

THE AQUARIUM SUN TERRACE, 1930. An unusual picture showing inset the Johnnie Walker sponsored Cricket Scoreboard. Cricket fans enjoyed watching the board each day, in this case, for the scores of the fourth test match taking place at Manchester. There is also a military parade in the picture, attracting a big crowd of spectators.

THE AQUARIUM, 1931. This shows the new entrance after the removal of the clock tower: just one of the many changes in the building and its fortunes through the years. During the Second World War it was used by the RAF, and when it was reopened it housed chimpanzee's tea parties, a motor museum, and, from 1968, dolphins. In 1991 the Dolphinarium was replaced by the Sea Life Centre.

THE AQUARIUM BY NIGHT. In the early years of this century, the attractions included such diverse creatures as a large octopus, sea-lions, alligators, and a live Norwegian lobster. My own particular memory of the aquarium in my childhood, is of a huge dead whale which had been washed up on Brighton Beach and which was exhibited for a short time in the building. I remember leaving that day, proudly clutching a model of Archie the Alligator, which had been procured for me by my father.

ROUGH SEAS, *c.* 1912. No collection of old Brighton pictures would be complete without a couple which illustrate the elements doing their worst. The message on this card refers to the sea being 'as rough as it can be, dashing over the breakwaters with huge splashes.' Many years at the start of the twentieth century were described by journalists as 'The worst in living memory'. 1912 brought severe gales in March, although primroses were gathered at Christmas.

ROUGH SEA AT PALACE PIER. The South Coast saw particularly bad weather in 1910. Brighton had its fair share as usual, and not far away Pagham Harbour, which had been reclaimed in 1876, was returned by the elements to its original state in the course of a few hours. At Selsey, the light railway was almost completely destroyed and was not reinstated until the following year.

19

THE GRAND HOTEL, early twentieth century. Probably Brighton's most famous hotel (although others may dispute this), it was built on the site of the old battery house and ammunition grounds and opened in 1864. An advertisement of 1929 spoke of its 250 bedrooms, with inclusive terms from thirteen shillings and sixpence a day. It was one of the first hotels to be fitted with a lift, which was described as 'an ascending omnibus.'

THE METROPOLE HOTEL. This picture is from around the same period as the one above. The Metropole was even larger than the Grand, with a colour scheme that clashed with the monochrome effect of the rest of Brighton's front. The architect was Alfred Waterhouse, who designed the Natural History Museum in London. This card was sent from the hotel itself, and signed by the housekeeper, E. Sharpe, who asks Mrs Rogers of Upper Russell Street if she or her daughter will 'come in at 6 o'clock Sunday morning to begin several weeks' work.'

INTERIOR OF METROPOLE HOTEL. The card is postmarked 1916, but the picture looks very 'pre-First World War'. An old advertisement says the hotel offers dancing to the New Metronome Six and there certainly appear to be six musicians in this picture. The message on the reverse says, 'Dancing the other night has properly done for Hubert', so perhaps the music was too jazzy for him.

THE METROPOLE HOTEL. Another picture, this time definitely dated 1903. Added interest is provided by the pedestrians and vehicles in the foreground.

THE OLD SHIP HOTEL, c. 1845. This very well known Brighton hostelry has a long history, stretching back to the days, possibly in Elizabethan times, when it was known simply as The Ship. When a second Ship Hotel appeared opposite the original, it was forced to change its name to The Old Ship. Local historian Clifford Musgrave said that it probably aquired its original name because it was constructed, at least in part, from the timbers of an old sailing vessel. A piece of carved wood, apparently part of a ship, once formed a section of the stable entrance.

ROYAL ALBION HOTEL AND ROUGH SEA, c. 1909. This is another of Brighton's many well-known hotels. Designed by A.H. Wilds, the building was opened in 1826. Originally merely the 'Albion', it became known as 'Royal' in about 1847.

KINGS ROAD, *c.* 1913. This important road was opened by King George IV on 29 January 1822, his way strewn with sugar plums – an old Brighton custom. A poem extolling life on the road in the early 1900s, shows that travel affected all segments of Brighton's population, from nursemaids and a blind guitarist, to demure nuns and a charabanc on its way to The Dyke.

MADEIRA WALK, early 1900s. This elegant promenade below Madeira Terrace was immediately popular with young and old alike. It is supported by cast iron columns, appropriately adorned with figures of Neptune and Aphrodite.

EAST CLIFF, c. 1930. Brighton seafront is dominated by massive cliffs, rising to around 80 feet above the sea and protected, from the 1830s, by a massive sea wall with an unsurpassed frontage along Marine Parade. Since 1908 this has also been known as King's Cliff, in honour of Edward VII, who often stayed in Brighton.

QUEEN VICTORIA STATUE, VICTORIA GARDENS. Designed by Nicoli, this statue was presented to the town by Sir John Blaker at the opening of the Gardens, at the time of the Queen's Diamond Jubilee in 1897. This photograph probably dates from shortly after the statue was erected.

THE OLD STEINE, late 1800s. The Victoria Fountain in the picture was erected in 1846 to mark the Queen's twenty-seventh birthday. Local musician Charles Coate composed *The Fountain Quadrille* to mark the event.

THE OLD STEINE AND NURSEMAIDS, *c.* 1905. Originally an ill-drained area of land, local fishermen considered it to be their own and used it to dry nets and store boats. In 1776 it was enclosed, much to their disgust. By 1785, the Prince Regent was going dove shooting here and hitting several chimney pots, either by accident or design.

BRIGHTON WAR MEMORIAL, 1920s. Located in the northern part of The Old Steine, the war memorial was unveiled in 1922 by Earl Beatty. A statue of George IV which originally stood on the site was removed to the North Gate of the Royal Pavilion.

SOUTH ENTRANCE TO THE ROYAL PAVILION, *c. 1990.* Undoubtedly Brighton's most famous building, with many thousands of words being applied both for and against it. Byron wrote, 'Shut up the King – no, the Pavilion; Lest it will cost us another million', echoing many voices at the time. Happily, the town bought it in 1850 for £53,000 and it has delighted most visitors and residents ever since.

THE BANQUETING ROOM, THE ROYAL PAVILION, *c.* 1907. Shown in this picture is the giant chandelier, weighing over a ton. The great kitchen which served the dining hall was added to the building in 1815. A visitor in 1818 wrote of the many contrivances for 'roasting, boiling, baking, stewing, frying, steaming and heating.' The Prince Regent visiting the kitchen one day found his favourite 'Dipper' Martha Gunn, secreting a pack of butter under her capacious gown. He gradually edged her nearer to the ovens, so that the heat would melt the butter. The result can be imagined.

THE DOME, late 1800s. Originally the Royal Pavilion stables, it housed 44 horses, with their ostlers and grooms. Construction of the building commenced in 1803, and it was converted to a concert hall around 1867, reopening as a magnificent Assembly Hall capable of housing 2,500 people. On 6 April 1974, it played host to the Eurovision Song Contest, won that year by ABBA with *Waterloo*.

WOUNDED INDIANS IN PAVILION GROUNDS, PLAYING CARDS. During the First World War, the Royal Pavilion and The Dome were used as an Indian military hospital. The first patients were admitted in December 1914, and a total of 4,306 passed through the 724 bed hospital.

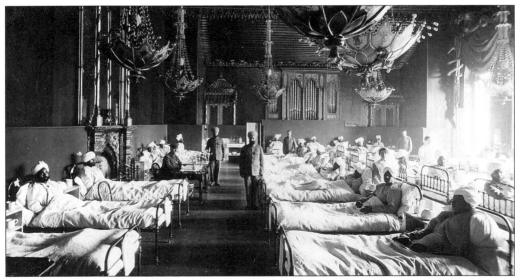

WARD FIVE OF THE ROYAL PAVILION HOSPITAL (THE MUSIC ROOM). The Indian patients felt very much at home in the Eastern atmosphere of the Pavilion. One of the ornate chandeliers above the beds weighed 1.75 tons and had 520 gas jets. An Indian soldier waking in his Pavilion bed, fell back with a seraphic smile, uttering the words 'Allah be praised, I have entered Paradise.'

CONVALESCENT GURKHAS IN THE PAVILION GROUNDS, FIRST WORLD WAR. With the Royal Pavilion functioning as an Indian war hospital, catering must have been a headache for the cooks, with no beef for the Hindus, no pork or bacon for the Muslims and a different kitchen and water supply for each.

ROYAL HIGHLANDERS IN THE ROYAL PAVILION DURING THE FIRST WORLD WAR. From 20 April 1916 to 21 July 1919, the Pavilion became a general army hospital with 6,085 admissions. On 28 August 1920, the military authorities relinquished control of the Pavilion hospital.

THE FLORAL HALL, c. 1929. This was built in 1900 and formed part of a new wholesale fruit and vegetable market. At the southern end there was the colourful Floral Hall, dedicated entirely to the sale of flowers. The whole market closed in 1938.

REGENCY SQUARE, early 1900s. This impressive collection of buildings appeared between 1818 and 1828, on the site of Bell View Field. This had been a favourite place for fairs, with a large capstan in the centre. It was reputedly haunted by the ghost of Betsy Bedlam in the eighteenth century, and was also the site of Brighton West Mill, which on 28 March 1797 was transported by sledge up the Dyke Road to a new site.

THE COLONNADE, *c.* 1906. Once rejoicing in the name 'The Royal Colonnade', it was built in 1806/7 and extended in 1827. In this picture it is the home of Homer Herring – a well-known Brighton hat and mantle business. (The term 'mantle' used to mean a sleeveless garment. The word vanished from common usage in the 1920s.) The area once had a very doubtful reputation, for it was popular with prostitutes late at night, after the theatre and music hall had closed.

THE ROYAL ALEXANDRA HOSPITAL FOR SICK CHILDREN, late 1800s. The hospital was founded by Dr R.P.B. Taafe in Western Road in 1868, and moved to Dyke Road in 1871. The girls' ward was named The Taafe Ward in honour of the founder. In 1954, the present Princess Alexandra became the hospital's patron.

THE LANES, EARLY THIS CENTURY. This picture shows part of a series of twittens (a Sussex dialect word for narrow passages), in the heart of the old town. The area, once known as The Hempshares, was developed in the sixteenth and seventeenth centuries, with most existing buildings dating from the eighteenth and nineteenth centuries. Until the 1930s, the Lanes were considered shabby and there were plans afoot to build modern shops on the site, but in the mid-1970s they suddenly became fashionable. Meeting House Lane was said to be haunted by a nun, who had been walled up for eloping with a soldier. Dressed in a grey habit, she was said to move through a built-up archway. Anyone who glimpsed her face was doomed.

BRIGHTON'S FIRST BELISHA BEACON, 1935. This was in Western Road, and was the first in the town of the now-familiar natty black-and-white striped poles with the orange ball on top. Named after the then Transport Minister, Leslie Hore-Belisha, they were a not unsuccessful attempt to make the ever increasing motor traffic give way to the poor pedestrian. In the picture, there is a sign advertising the new International Stores as the finest grocery and provision store on the South Coast.

BLACK ROCK, 1930s. Probably named after a particular rock or cave that lay at the bottom of the cliffs, this marked the point where the white chalk of the South Downs reached the sea. It was Brighton's eastern boundary since the seventeenth century and remained so until 1928.

LANDSLIP AT BLACK ROCK. This was one of many in the 1920s. After the landslips, the usual way to the beach was through the sweet shop next to the inn, for which a charge of a penny was made. In 1824, a tunnel was made to the gas works, but was bricked up in 1850. In 1906, Magnus Volk reopened the south end, calling it a 'Smugglers Cave'. In 1932, a new 60ft-wide road between Black Rock and Rottingdean was opened and the Abergavenny Arms inn was demolished.

THE SWIMMING POOL, BLACK ROCK, 1930s. Opened in 1936, this was a highly popular pool, 165 ft by 60 ft, with handsome changing rooms and cafe. I can well remember the happy sounds from the pool whenever I passed by. It was closed in 1978, amid much disappointment, and the site left for future development.

QUEEN'S PARK LAKE, early 1900s. Renamed Queen's Park after Queen Adelaide in 1836, it started life in 1824 as Brighton Park. Attractions included an aviary and roller-skating rink. The latter was eventually converted into an ornamental lake, fed by an artificial cascade and stream. A tree planted nearby on 6 August 1985 carried the message 'never again', to mark those killed by atomic bombs forty years earlier.

QUEEN'S PARK, c. 1910. Another view of the lake, this time featuring 'A gallant rescue', which was almost certainly posed for the cameraman, with no shortage of young 'extras'.

QUEENS ROAD, 1902. This major road was built in 1845 to provide ready access to the railway station from the middle of the town. The London, Brighton and South Coast Railway Company contributed £2,000 to the cost, which included the bridge over Trafalgar Street. The road was widened in 1878, and again in 1935. Many will remember it with mixed feelings, as it was in a building along Queen's Road that conscripts in the Second World War were given their initial medicals.

DYKE ROAD, early 1900s. Until the nineteenth century, Dyke Road was a main route to Brighton from the North. Many famous people lived here, including Dame Flora Robson and the local engineer and inventor Magnus Volk. Note the forlorn apple lady waiting for customers on the right of the photograph.

EAST STREET, early 1900s. A dream-like picture on what must have been a busy day at the time. By the mid-nineteenth century this was a densely populated area of the town, with a gateway leading down into Pool Valley. Formerly called Great East Street, it is still one of the most important shopping streets in Brighton. Here also stood The Rising Sun inn, haunted by a ghost known as Old Strike-a-Light. The inn was originally called The Naked Boy and carried a sign of a naked child bearing the inscription, 'So fickle is our English nation, I would be clothed if I knew the fashion.'

TRAFALGAR STREET, early 1900s. In this photograph of a street developed after the railway arrived in the 1840s, the pedestrians pause to watch the photographer. It is now on the edge of the North Laines Conservation Area, which is becoming popular because of its wealth of unusual and specialist shops.

KEMP TOWN FROM THE AIR, mid-1900s. Although the original Kemp Town was an estate built by Thomas Read Kemp from 1823, the name is now applied to that part of Brighton east of Rock Gardens. Thomas Read Kemp was born on 23 December 1782, becoming an MP and also the founder of a religious sect at St James Chapel, Brighton, in 1816. He died in 1844 in Paris, and there is a tablet to his memory in St Nicholas's church.

ROMAN CATHOLIC CHURCH OF ST JOHN THE BAPTIST, KEMP TOWN. Built in 1836, on the site of a small chapel, St John the Baptist was only the fourth Roman Catholic church to be built in England since the Reformation. Mrs Fitzherbert is buried here. In her old age she made this her church, coming every Saturday after it had closed, knowing that the Irish priest had instructed the charlady to let her in. He is supposed to have said, 'And when you see her out, ye'll bob her a curtsy, for maybe she's the rightful Queen of England – and maybe she's not.'

ST PETER'S CHURCH, *c.* 1905. This has been Brighton's parish church since 1873. It was built originally in 1824/8 as a chapel of ease to St Nicholas's church at a total cost of £20,365.

ST NICHOLAS'S CHURCH, EARLY 1900s. This was the ancient parish church of Brighton, dedicated to St Nicholas, patron saint of fishermen. Many supernatural beliefs are associated with the church and churchyard. These include a ghostly white horse and rider, and a spectral ship which was watched for from the churchyard by a Lady Edona, whose lover was returning from the Crusades. The song *St Nicholas's Lament* says a lot about the feelings aroused by the church's loss of status in 1873. One verse must suffice: 'But now I am growing old, neglected and forgot. My walls are all damaged, my timbers left to rot. When ere a church rates made, St Peter's gets it all, for useless decorations, whilst I in ruin fall'.

BRIGHTON SHOWHOUSE, *c.* 1942. The back of this postcard says, 'Don't miss this opportunity of obtaining a seaside home worth £1,000 free of all cost... also a wonderful investment by making an initial payment of £1. To visitors – take train to Brighton station. Frequent bus service from the Aquarium to Saltdean.'

PYLONS, ('THE GATEWAY TO BRIGHTON'), 1934. Standing at the northern limit of greater Brighton, these were designed by John L. Denman, and the foundation stone laid by the Duke and Duchess of York on 30 May 1928. Buried inside are coins, Brighton newspapers, and a book about the foundation stone ceremony. Many will probably share my own childhood memories of repeating, 'We're not in Brighton, we're not in Brighton' as the pylons came in sight from the bus, and then triumphantly changing to, 'We are in Brighton' at the crucial moment.

Two

Hove

THE LAWNS, HOVE, *c.* 1910. Brighton long had its sights trained on neighbouring Hove, desiring municipal wedlock. But Hove persistently 'played hard to get'. Even the guide books had to recognise the difference between the two towns, with descriptions of 'Brighton Prom', contrasting with those of 'Hove Lawns'.

BRIGHTON AND HOVE BOUNDARY AND PEACE STATUE, 1929. Brighton had extended its boundaries on many occasions in order to accommodate new buildings and developments outside the original area of the town. But Hove has always resisted such advances, determined to keep a physical boundary between the two places.

THE KING EDWARD VII PEACE STATUE, early 1900s. The elegant statue is of an angel of peace, 30 ft tall, standing on a sphere supported by four dolphins. It was unveiled on 12 October 1912 and was to commemorate the provision of a home for the Queen's Nurses in Brighton, which was opened on the same day.

THE BOUNDARY, *c.* 1908. Hove, Brighton's western neighbour, started life as a small village. Although the expression of 'Hove, actually' has become a local joke, the town certainly had a completely different character to its larger twin and was well known for its beautiful lawns, gardens and fashionable buildings and society. But Hove is by no means ashamed of its earlier history, which includes such things as smuggling and prize fighting.

HOVE PROMENADE . Nº 25.

HOVE SEAFRONT AND GARDENS, early 1900s. The gardens, for which Hove is noted, provide an attractive alternative to Brighton's more commercialised prom. Notwithstanding its fairly staid image, an Easter Monday game of 'Kiss in the Ring' was once played annually in Hove, and not only by children. One man told me with relish how it provided a useful excuse to get to know members of the opposite sex, until Victorian disapproval put an end to such capers.

Queen's Gardens, Hove, showing the late King Edward's Favourite Seat.

KING EDWARD'S FAVOURITE SEAT, early 1900s. Edward VII visited Brighton and Hove many times and when he was 59 came here in an attempt to help his bronchitis. He was friendly with the Sassoon family and often stayed with Arthur Sassoon at King's Gardens, Hove. This picture also provides a lovely view of an invalid carriage, so typical of the time and place.

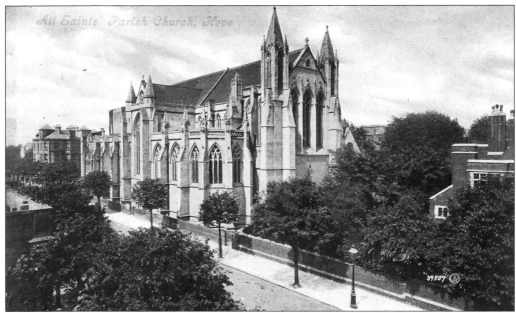

All Saints' Parish Church, Hove

HOVE PARISH CHURCH, *c.* 1906. Dedicated to All Saints, the foundation stone was laid in 1899, although it was many years before the church was fully completed.

Hove Street, Part of Old Hove where smuggling, Bull-baiting, Cock Fighting and Prize Fighting used to take place.

HOVE STREET. A turn of the century postcard view with no wheeled vehicles in sight. Some of Hove's less respectable history is mentioned on the card, with a statement that smuggling, bull baiting, cock fighting and prize fighting all took place in this area of the town. Cock fighting was certainly very popular in both Brighton and Hove and contests were advertised regularly in Sussex newspapers. Even more unacceptable by modern standards were such things as cock throwing, 'Cock-in-the-pot' and 'Thrashing the Hen', details of which are best left to the imagination.

Paddling on the Sands at Hove.

PADDLING ON THE SANDS, *c.* 1918. Hove was popular not only with adults, but also with children, because of the serene atmosphere of the seaside.

HOVE TOWN HALL, late 1800s. Built in 1852, at a cost of £50,000, this was generally regarded as a splendid edifice. The grand hall was 90 ft by 60 ft, had three balconies, and held 2,000 people. The tower *carillon* played 14 different tunes, including *Home, Sweet Home, Auld Land Syne*, and *Rule Brittania*. The Town Hall was devastated by a great fire on Sunday 9 January 1966, after which it was replaced by a new building.

CHURCH ROAD, *c.* 1905. This is one of Hove's most important roads, featuring many of its best buildings, including the old Town Hall seen on the left. Margaret Powell in her entertaining book *Below Stairs*, remembered Hove as, 'a wonderful place, especially for children… Immediately behind the town was the country. We only had to walk a matter of minutes from where we lived and there was the country and the farms'.

SUSSEX ROOM, HOVE MUSEUM, mid-1900s. The Sussex Room included such bygone objects as the yokes of Sussex ox teams. It was discontinued in 1966, when the Hove museum was used as a temporary Town Hall, after a fire at the real Town Hall. All the furniture in the Sussex room was then sold. The present curator says that this is the one feature of the museum displays of pre-1966 Hove which almost all visitors of a certain age remember and enquire about.

POLICE SEASIDE HOME, c. 1915. The original building was the first of its kind in England. After a few years it was found to be too small and a new bigger home was built in Portland Road, at a cost of £9,210. Work continued at a new building in Kingsway, which was opened in 1966.

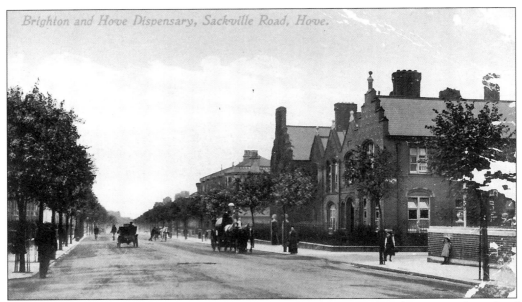

DISPENSARY, SACKVILLE ROAD, early 1900s. This was opened as the western branch of the Brighton Dispensary on 3 December 1888, to the sound of the hymn *Thou to Whom the Sick and Dying*. Finance was difficult in the early days, but in the 1920s it was the first hospital in Sussex to have its own Radium for treating cancer.

NEW PARK, HOVE, SHOWING GOLDSTONE, DRUIDS ALTAR.

THE GOLDSTONE, HOVE PARK, mid-1930s. This sarsen stone was causing annoyance to a local farmer. He employed labourers to bury it and there it stayed forgotten until 1906 when it was relocated by William Holcombe to Hove Park. Tradition says that it was one of the stones moved by the Devil when he created Devil's Dyke. Some claim that a face may be discovered on the stone when viewed in a certain light.

PRINT OF ST ANN'S WELL, late nineteenth century. This was a chalybeate spring said to be named after Lady Annefrida, whose tears at the death of her betrothed Wolnuth, caused the well to erupt. The pump room was built around the spring in the late nineteenth century. Dr Russell recommended it to his patients, although locals already knew its reputation. The well house was demolished in 1935 and the well covered.

ST ANN'S WELL GARDENS, mid 1900s. Originally part of the Wick Estate, it became a garden around 1850. By the turn of the century, it was being run by a private syndicate as pleasure grounds boasting refreshments, swing boats, fireworks, and Mrs Lee – a Gypsy fortune teller.

HOVE PRIVATE SCHOOL, c. 1899. The name and location of the school are unknown, but the lady who provided the picture recalls that her grandfather was the lovely little boy on the left with the curls. This was evidently one of the many private schools in Hove and Brighton which flourished during this period.

PORTLAND ROAD SCHOOL, HOVE, c. 1913. This is a contrast to the above picture. It was sent as a Christmas card and was inscribed on the reverse, 'With the compliments of the season from…' Also handwritten is the comment, 'A beloved class and self.' The latter must have been one of the two teachers standing at the back – probably the young lady.

Three
Around and About

INDIAN WAR MEMORIAL, PATCHAM, *c.* 1922. This memorial, known as the Chattri, was erected on the site of the funeral pyres of the Indian soldiers (Sikhs and Gurkhas) who died from wounds in the Pavilion Hospital during the First World War. The bodies were taken by motor hearse to this spot on the Downs, placed on concrete slabs surrounded by logs to a height of about 3 ft, and then burnt. Some of the ashes were thrown into the sea and others sent to relatives in India.

PRESTON ROAD, *c.* 1916. The road runs through Preston parish from Preston Circus to London Road, Patcham. There was a turnpike gate at Preston, and the Crown and Anchor in Preston village was the first stop for coaches outside Brighton.

PRESTON, *c.* 1904. Among the old buildings was a farmhouse later used as a tea-room. The tiny Preston Workhouse also existed up to 1844. Brighton was once said to be tree-less, but this description could by no means apply to the entrance to the town via Preston.

FIRE AT ST PETER'S CHURCH, PRESTON, 23 June 1906. The church dates from the thirteenth century and was restored in 1870 and again in 1906 following the fire. Sadly, some fine mural paintings of the fourteenth century were damaged in the fire.

PRESTON PARK, *c.* 1910. The park extends to 63 acres and was purchased in 1883 from the Bennett-Stanford family of Preston Manor. In 1928 the park was remodelled and is Brighton's largest ornamental open space. The writer of the postcard was completely unimpressed by its allure, preferring instead to go to the picture palace 'with my Percy'.

LOVER'S WALK, PRESTON PARK, late nineteenth century. Lover's walk was once a tree-lined path with romantic associations until in 1831 it was connected with an infamous murder case. John Holloway carried the remains of his wife to the Walk and buried her there. After his trial and execution, she was re-buried in Preston Church.

THE MEADOW, OVINGBEAN.

MEADOW AT OVINGDEAN, *c.* 1926. This picture is a reminder of the days when the countryside around Brighton was synonomous with sheep farming. However, young James, who sent the card to Alice in London, was more interested in telling her that he had been to the cinema and seen a film with lumber, dams and fighting.

OVINGDEAN GRANGE, *c.* 1910. This was the old manor house of the village and has a place in literary annals as the title of a book by Harrison Ainsworth about a fictitious visit by King Charles II in 1651. Probably few people read Ainsworth's books today, but they were once best-sellers. My copy carries a prize book-plate stating that it was awarded as first prize at St Augustines, Brighton, in 1934 and is signed by the local vicar.

ROTTINGDEAN AND THE HANGMAN'S STONE. This undated photograph shows Rottingdean windmill in the distance. Well known as the logo of the publishers Heinemann, the windmill was built in 1802 and preserved largely by the efforts of the Sussex author Hilaire Belloc. It was said to have been used by smugglers for signalling to each other. The old gentleman is sitting on The Hangman's Stone, which legend says was the scene of a sheep stealer being strangled with his own rope.

THE CLIFFS, ROTTINGDEAN. A charming early 1900s picture of a seaside cafe, with just enough patrons to keep it in business, but not enough to spoil the quietness.

ROTTINGDEAN VILLAGE STREET, *c.* 1904. This dates from a time when Sussex roads were used mainly by walkers. Note the children with their iron hoops, probably made for them by the local blacksmith (who, about this time, was a Mr Edward Sanders). Many local surnames survive in Rottingdean. An old song says 'We have Sussex names in plenty. There's Sexby, Allwork, Henty, and Dudeneys, and Moppetts right and left'.

ROTTINGDEAN VILLAGE STREET, AN UNDATED PICTURE, POSSIBLY FROM THE LATE NINETEENTH CENTURY. The locals are obviously fascinated by the photographer. Artists and authors, such as Rudyard Kipling, Sir Edward Burne-Jones, Conan Doyle, William Blake and Hilaire Belloc, have always felt at home here. The village is still popular with theatrical and artistic personalities.

WHITE HORSE INN, ROTTINGDEAN, early 1900s. A vegetable cart waits for business, while two horse riders proceed leisurely up the uncluttered street. A two-horse bus, driven by Walter Holden (known as 'Scribbets') left twice daily from the inn for Brighton. The village boys marked its leaving with the cry of 'There goes the rabbit hutch.' The writer of the postcard has added beneath the inn 'Is this where C. gets his milk for breakfast'.

RUDYARD KIPLING'S HOUSE, c. 1906. The children show off their home-made go-cart, disregarding the fame attached to the house behind them. Kipling wrote the *Just so* stories whilst at Rottingdean, but eventually decided he could not stand the visitors who came out from Brighton on the bus to obtain a sight of him.

SIR EDWARD BURNE-JONES'S HOUSE, early 1900s. North End House, opposite the Green, was the home of the famous painter, who now rests in the church alongside his wife. He designed much of the stained-glass in the church.

ROTTINGDEAN POND, early 1900s. This ancient pond once contained carp, but at the time of this picture, village children used to love to sail their toy boats, and do other juvenile things, on it. It was also used by shepherds for watering their flocks and by a local carter. One day his horse and cart got stuck in the mud and to the amusement of the bystanders he took off his trousers and used them as a whip.

PORTSLADE HARVEST THANKSGIVING, 1917. This was in the local Salvation Army Hall and shows how the church organisations were taking over the harvest festivities from the farmers and landowners. Portslade still had the character of a village at this time. Not long before it had a 'Wise Woman' known as Granny Rumney. She had long legs and would stride along the muddy roads wearing Sussex 'pattens'. Small boys would call after her, 'Here's Granny Rumney on her pattens. Fast as she goes, her tongue goes clacken'.

CHILDREN IN NATIONAL COSTUME, ST NICHOLAS SCHOOL, PORTSLADE, 1911. This was at the school's celebrations for the coronation of King George V. At this time, teachers loved to see their children dressed in national costumes and usually celebrated the very popular Empire Day in this manner.

ST ANDREWS' CHURCH, PORTSLADE, 25 April 1908. In late April 1908, winter returned to Sussex, with a severe snowstorm lasting two hours. At Brighton, spring flowers were buried by snow, and traffic was severely affected. Christmas the same year also had very bad weather, with the Brighton tramway service having to be suspended.

VILLAGE STREET, FALMER, c. 1905. An archetypal village scene, full of peace and quiet in the years preceding the First World War. There has been a village here since before Domesday, containing a very old pond, which, before it was partly filled in, was noted for its depth. The writer Godfrey Winn lived in Mill House, until he died in 1971.

THE DEVIL'S DYKE HOTEL, *c.* 1909. James Henry Hubbard was a nineteenth-century entrepreneur who ran a hotel and teahouse at the beauty spot close to Brighton known as the Dyke. He quickly added swings, roundabouts, coconut shies, a shooting gallery and a brass band. One Whit Monday at the height of his success, he had 30,000 visitors.

THE DEVIL'S DYKE CANNON, early 1900s. This was one of Mr Hubbard's many attractions: a wooden cannon, which supplemented other things such as a cable railway, and a steep funicular. His slogan was, 'A real rest from the bustle of business', which seems singularly unbelievable.

DENNETT'S CORNER TEA SHOP, *c.* 1900. Mr John Dennett ran this tea shop, by arrangement with Mr Hubbard, near the railway station at the Dyke. On Sundays, the little trains brought thousands of visitors and the band played in a grove of trees.

GYPSY FORTUNE TELLER AT DEVIL'S DYKE, *c.* 1912. One more of Mr Hubbard's many ideas for attracting coppers from his visitors. The caravan looks genuine enough, although its travelling days were probably over.

THE TRUE LEGEND OF THE DEVIL'S DYKE. (1)

'TWAS ev'ning in the realms Below,
The Eternal Fire a great red glow ;
When Satan, caught with Wanderlust,

Resolved to take a stroll, just
To demoralise the World without —
The World he'd heard so much about.

THE LEGEND OF THE DYKE. Long before Mr Hubbard and his fairground gimmicks appeared on the scene, local folk were familiar with the legendary origins of the Dyke. A well-known Sussex folk story tells how the Devil tried to drown the little Christian churches of the Sussex Weald, but was prevented from accomplishing his wicked plan by the forces of goodness. This card is the first of a series produced in the early 1900s, giving one version of the legend in rhyme.

THE TRUE LEGEND OF THE DEVIL'S DYKE. (6)

With an awful oath Nick hurriedly fled ;
What seemed Success was Failure instead.
He firmly resolved to make no more raids,

But in future would stay in peaceful Hades.
There never was a gruesome tale like
The true Legend of ''THE DEVIL'S DYKE.''

THE LEGEND OF THE DYKE. The final card in the series, proving that Old Nick was unable to get the better of true Sussex folk.

THE DEVIL'S DYKE RAILWAY STATION, *c.* 1909. The railway ran from 1887. It left the main Brighton line at Hove, passing close by Hangleton church, with the terminus at the Dyke. The carriage on the left of the picture was a buffet room run by a retired guard.

DEVILS DYKE STATION, April 1936. The end of the railway came in 1938, with a crowd of 350 to say farewell to 'The Dyke Express'. This picture taken just two years earlier has an air of poignancy, as by that time the line was running with an ever decreasing number of passengers.

FULKING VILLAGE, *c.* 1912. At the start of the nineteenth century there were said to be 2,600 sheep in the parish of Fulking, with only 258 humans. For this reason, sheep and Fulking were closely linked. The local inn is aptly named the Shepherd and Dog, and many shepherds took their sheep to be washed in the clear spring water that rises here. The main road, which ran through the sheep washing area was closed – but then this probably only involved a handful of carts.

THE HAUNTED LAKE AT DEVILS DYKE, NEAR POYNINGS. In 1883 three boys were bathing in the lake and one got into difficulties and drowned. One of the survivors is said to haunt the lake, having died of melancholia after failing to rescue his friend.

Four

Work...

THE FISH MARKET, *c.* 1908. Brighton's principal centres of employment were on the sea and in the fields. Fishing had gone on at Brighton beach for centuries – in fact, the town was a fishing village long before it was discovered by fashionable society. This is one of a series of postcards showing the activity at the sea-front fish market: activity which intensified whenever the large fishing smacks arrived loaded with fish.

INTENDED HOVE FISHERY, *c.* 1814. A print of a suggested development at Hove in the early part of the nineteenth century, which was to include dwellings for sixty fishermen. It is interesting to note that grandiose schemes are not just a phenomenon of the present day!

LANDING MACKEREL, early twentieth century. Until the end of the nineteenth century, the height of the mackerel season was in June. At the start, every master of a fishing boat held a party on the beach. This custom was known as 'bending in' or 'bread, cheese and beer day'. It was said to have originated in pre-Reformation times, when the priest came to the beach to give Holy Communion to the men and their families. 'Bending in' is a corruption of 'benediction'.

Compliments
of the
Season, 1903

BRIGHTON
POLICE
FIRE
BRIGADE.

Superintendent :
L. V. LACROIX.

NEW MOTOR.

BRIGHTON FIRE ENGINE, 1903. A Christmas Greetings postcard showing off the Police and Fire Brigade's 'new motor'. Albert Paul in his book *Poverty-hardship but happiness* (1974) writes, 'Captain Lacroix would smash his way through doors and windows with his axe, sometimes, it was said, doing more damage than the fire.' He was the first holder of the Mayoral car number CD1, and was in charge of the fire brigade until 1921.

FIRE AT ABBEY'S BREWERY, 1907. Postcard manufacturers loved to put fires on their cards, but ordinary photographs seldom did them justice. A certain amount of imagination was therefore used (as with this picture). Brighton has always been noted for its vast number of pubs and beer houses, and consequently for its breweries, of which this was one.

HOVE FIRE BRIGADE, c. 1909. A splendid turn-out to celebrate either a local or a national event. Most brigades could not run to their own horses at this time, but had to rely on borrowed ones, which of course added to the time taken for the brigade's engine to reach the fire.

Old Water Well & Treadwheel Saddlescombe, Sussex, Was worked by one pony for 26 years

TREADWELL AT SADDLESCOMBE. A picture from early this century, demonstrating how a pony, by working the wheel, could bring water to the surface.

TAMPLIN'S BREWERY, 1934. The lovely sight of Tamplin's horses in the brewery yard. Shortly after this picture was taken, the horse-drawn carts were replaced by motor lorries. Now breweries are once again using heavy horses for deliveries and for publicity.

SERGEANT'S MESS, PATCHAM CAMP, 1913. This photograph was taken only months away from the spark that set European civilisation alight. Are the flowers on the tables simply for the benefit of the photographer?

BRANDY BALLS SELLER, late nineteenth century. There were apparently several brandy balls sellers in Brighton during the nineteenth century. My mother remembered one known as 'The Brandy Ball Man', who's call was 'Brandy Balls as big as St Pauls. Who will buy my Brandy Balls?' In the 1880s, one brandy balls seller was called 'Old Dizzy' because of his resemblance to Disraeli. This man's call was, 'Oh, they are beautiful today ladies, they are so fine'.

CHESTNUT SELLER, 1934. Good value at two-pence a bag. The chestnut seller's pitch was the corner of Church Street and Regent Street. Many of the 1930s street sellers were Italians, selling Hokey-Pokey (a type of ice-cream) in the summer and roast chestnuts in the winter.

SHEEP SHEARING AT FULKING, BEFORE 1912. This was at Perching Manor Farm. The man in the long coat and bowler hat is Mr Napthale (Nap) Page of Perching, a well-known local farmer who died in 1912. Note the seated spectators, especially the one with his jug of liquid joy.

STEAM THRESHING AT WOODINGDEAN, 1920s. The foreman of the gang was probably Mr Edwards. The steam threshing gangs worked from farm to farm, providing a brief interlude of relative excitement in the otherwise fairly humdrum farming year.

SUSSEX OXEN AT FALMER.

OX BOY AND CART AT FALMER, early 1900s. The ox boy controlled his massive beasts with an ox goad (a thin hazel stick 8 ft 3 in long). Oxen were not shod when they worked solely on soft ground, but when required to go on the roads they were provided with flat iron plates one of which was nailed on each side of their cloven hooves with special nails.

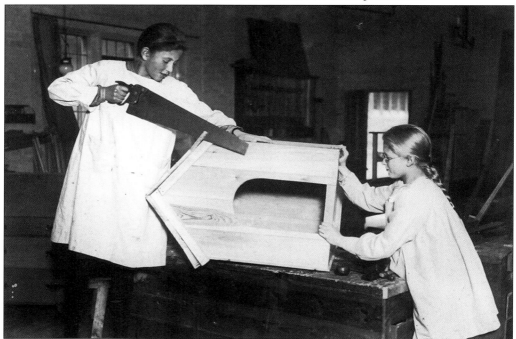

WOODWORK CLASS AT ROEDEAN SCHOOL, probably 1920s. This famous girls' school was founded in 1885 and began with ten pupils and no name. The school buildings at Roedean were opened in 1899, with much more being added in later years.

DOWNLAND SHEEP, NEAR BRIGHTON, *c.* 1908. The two characters in their straw boaters look a little out of place in this picture. Perhaps the photographer couldn't find a genuine shepherd to add to his picture. S.M. Moens in his charming history of Rottingdean (1952) gives a glimpse of a real Sussex shepherd, Steve Barrow, who died in 1926 at the age of 81, only a few months after he had persuaded a pilot to take him up in an aeroplane to loop-the-loop. When the hunt asked him one day if he had seen a fox, his reply was that he had been working too hard to notice.

THE SHEPHERD AND HIS SHEEP. An undated card, which clearly shows the strong connections between Brighton and shepherding which existed until the early years of this century.

SHEPHERD AND DOG ON DITCHLING BEACON, 1930s. By the 1930s, sheep and shepherds were still to be seen on the Downs, although in smaller numbers than at the start of the century. The shepherd's smock, umbrella and crook are no longer in evidence, although the dog is still a necessary companion.

SHEEP AT DEW POND, FALMER, 1920s. Many words have been used to describe these ponds and the manner in which they retain their water. Barclay Wills in his book on *Shepherds of Sussex* (1938) asked the shepherds themselves for their comments. One said, 'Well I reckon 'tis rain an mistes, but dont say as I said so!' Most shepherds in Sussex knew them as 'Ship-ponds', but in other counties they were called 'Mist-ponds', 'Cloud-ponds' or 'Fog-ponds'.

WEST BLATCHINGTON WINDMILL, 1930s. The mill, which was part of a thriving farm, dates from around 1820. In 1897 two of the sweeps blew down and the mill remained in a poor state for several years. The building features in some of the many tales about smuggling in relation to Sussex mills. It is said that the miller hid brandy and tobacco under sacks of meal, which were carried up to the mill in fishing nets.

WEST BLATCHINGTON WINDMILL, c. 1936. This picture was taken after the fire which destroyed the barn on the south side of the mill. The windmill was purchased by the Hove Corporation in 1937 with an agreement that it would be preserved. It was opened to the public in 1979 and over the years has undergone considerable restoration. Instead of farm buildings, it is now surrounded by housing estates.

CLAYTON MILLS NEAR BRIGHTON, 1930s. Although they are not far from Brighton, the reason these mills feature in this book is because 'Jill' (the white square post mill) was originally known as Hove Mill and was removed by sledge to Clayton in 1866, a team of oxen pulling it across the Downs. The other mill is, of course, named 'Jack'.

PATCHAM WINDMILL, 1920s. Built in 1884/5, this is said to be the last working windmill to be erected in Sussex. It can be seen from a long way away, so is well known, although not always by name. It stopped working in 1924 and was later converted into a dwelling house, with loving hands to care for it.

Five

... and Play

AN UNNAMED GROUP OF BRIGHTON MUSICIANS, late nineteenth century. An intriguing photograph, whose mystery perhaps some reader can solve. Among the instruments are violins, guitars and banjos, although several of the group seem to be non-players. The only clue is the photographer, T. Donovan of St James Street, Brighton, who was in business between 1879 and 1901.

JUBILEE DECORATIONS, THE CLOCK TOWER, 1935. These were for the Silver Jubilee of King George V. The Clock Tower built in 1888 was designed by John Johnson. It may be considered the hub of Brighton's shopping area. It cost £2,000, is 75 ft high, and is either a perfect piece of Victoriana, or, to quote Nairn and Pevsner in *The Buildings of England* (1965), 'Worthless.'

JUBILEE DECORATIONS,
LONDON ROAD, 1935.
Woolworth's threepenny and
sixpenny store may be seen in one of
Brighton's main shopping streets,
which was first developed in the
1810s and '20s, and widened in 1903.
The tram lines are also in evidence.

JUBILEE DECORATIONS, WEST
STREET, 1935. More decorations, this
time in what may have been part of
the fishermens' town, although by the
eighteenth century it was Brighton's
most exclusive street. It was widened
in 1928/38 and all the buildings on the
western side were moved, except for St
Paul's church, which may be seen on
the left. It is the shortest way to the sea
from the railway station.

THE WHEELER BAND, *c.* 1901. Well, not a very big band, but well enough known in the town to feature in a series of postcards of 'Brighton Celebrities'. The figures shown on this card were made into cardboard models by the artist Clem Lambert and displayed in Mr H. Willett's carvers and gilders shop at 39 Ship Street in the early 1900s.

PORTSLADE SALVATION ARMY BAND, *c.* 1910. Members of the band, all of whom were part of the same local family, in their best uniform. The Salvation Army was founded by William Booth in 1878 and during the 1880s and '90s, at Brighton and other south coast towns, his form of militant religion led to much violence and street fighting. (The windows of the Brighton HQ were smashed at this time.) Happily, by the early 1900s, such scenes had become part of the Sally's history.

PORTSLADE TOWN BAND, *c.* 1910. In this photograph, Peter Wynne is the bass drummer and Alfred Steele is second-from-the-left in the front row. Portslade merged with the borough of Hove in 1974, although for a long time it boasted a larger population of humans and animals than its neighbour. At the turn of the century it was not at all a poor relation to Hove, and was proud of its own institutions, such as the Town Band.

PORTSLADE SUNDAY SCHOOLS OUTING, 22 JULY 1914. This was the parade at the start of an outing to Hassocks by all the Sunday Schools in the area. The Salvation Army band led the way, followed by children and adults, apparently dressed in their best clothes. The Railway Inn is on the right of the photograph, so evidently the party were travelling by train. It is interesting to conjecture exactly how they spent their time when they arrived at Hassocks, which must have been a fairly sleepy place at that time.

BRIGHTON FRIENDLY AND TRADES SOCIETIES HOSPITAL SATURDAY COMMIT-
TEE, 1910. This was part of a parade organised by the committee on 16 July 1910. The old
voluntary hospitals depended largely on local financial support and funds raised by bodies such
as this.

FRENCH VISITORS, May 1907. *Entente cordiale* was alive and well in Brighton at this time,
when a group from the Comite du Commerce France paid a visit to the town. They were taken
on a motor bus tour and no doubt enjoyed the sight of the Royal Pavilion, which can be seen in
this photograph.

Coronation Day June 22 1911 Preston Park   Gilbert Nº 2

CORONATION DAY, PRESTON PARK, 22 June 1911. This was the coronation of George V, who was to be more closely associated with Bognor later in his life. Preston Park, as the largest of Brighton's parks, was used for many fetes and festivals such as this Coronation Day celebration. How well-dressed the people all appear.

PROCLAMATION OF KING GEORGE V 1910. BRIGHTON

PROCLAMATION OF THE ACCESSION OF KING GEORGE V, 1910. The formal proclamation in Brighton and the year before the coronation of the new King. Without present day mass communication, occasions such as this took on a much more vital role in local life.

CROWNING OF THE TEMPERANCE QUEEN, 1925. The temperance movement was very strong in the first half of this century. On the supposition that the Devil need not have all the best tunes, the movement had its own celebrations, including the crowning of a Temperance Queen. This took place in the Dome, with banners making such inspiring proclamations as, 'God is Love' and, 'Dare to be a Daniel'.

ELLISON'S ENTERTAINERS, 1914. One of the best known of the many groups of entertainers and musicians that performed in Brighton in the early years of this century.

H. BEE'S MERRIEFOLK, 1909. Another group who performed in the traditional seaside pierrot costumes on the Palace Pier. All the members have signed this postcard, which presumably would have been sold as a souvenir after the show.

JACK SHEPPARD'S ENTERTAINERS, 1927. Yet one more group of entertainers, who were very well known in Brighton at this time. They have forsaken the old pierrot costumes for much more stylish 1920s-style outfits.

THE HIGHWAYMEN, 1908. Their costumes fitted their name and they were evidently a very popular Brighton attraction, as this was a photograph marking their fourth season. They performed on a portable stage on the beach, in true seaside pierrot fashion.

CONCERT PARTY ON THE BEACH, early 1900s. Another group who performed on the beach, this time called The Cadets, displaying the type of portable stage in use at this time. For a modest fee the audience sat in deck-chairs, and others were invited to make a contribution when the 'bottler' came round. The postcard was given free with such publications as *Smart Novels* and *Yes or No*.

THE WHITE COONS, 1905. A well-known group who gave their performances close to the Metropole Hotel. They sported white suits and hats, and stiff 3 inch double collars. They were, of course, an English version of the popular American black-faced minstrels. Included in the company was the comedian Will Pepper.

PROFESSOR CYRIL'S CYCLE DIVE, c. 1908. One of the many attractions on the West Pier at this time. The Professor performed his daring cycle dive off the pier and into the sea, to the delight of the spectators.

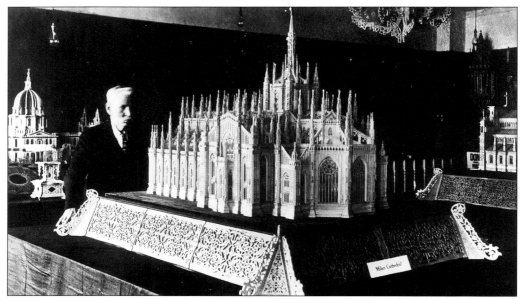

RICHARD OLD AND MODEL OF MILAN CATHEDRAL, 1930s. This was the no.1 exhibit in the Richold Collection exhibited on the West Pier at this time. It was described as the world's finest model, containing over 8,000 pieces. Mr Old finished it in 1898, having taken over five years to build it by oil lamplight on his kitchen table.

STANELLI. VIOLINIST AND COMPOSER, *c.* 1904. The message on the back of this postcard says, 'I saw this wonderful child on Saturday and was very much struck. He is simply a marvel. He was performing at the aquarium all last week.' Was he perhaps the same Stanelli who later starred in BBC radio Saturday Night Music Halls?

PROFESSOR HENO'S PROFESSIONAL CARD, early 1900s. The Professor was a Brighton conjuror, ventriloquist and Punch-and-Judy-Man. He performed both as a single act, and with his 'Funny Folks'.

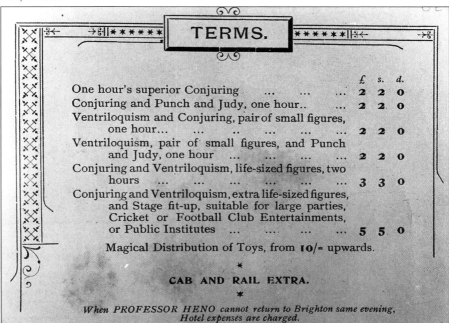

PROFESSOR HENO'S TERMS. This is the reverse side of the card shown above. By modern standards, Professor Heno's terms appear very reasonable, although he did warn his patrons that cab and rail fares were extra, and hotel expenses would be charged for more distant bookings.

GATHERING WILD FLOWERS NEAR BRIGHTON, 1936. This is a very unsophisticated picture from the '30s. Brighton's children had for years been picking wild flowers and making them into garlands for May Day. In 1771, the Prince of Macklenburg-Strelitz, who was staying at Brighton for his health, was presented with these garlands, and gave each of the little girls involved half a guinea.

THE BIJOU ELECTRIC EMPIRE CINEMA, *c.* 1913. Although it opened in 1911 with the above name, it will be remembered by many as a news cinema. It was a wonderful and inexpensive way to spend a little spare time whilst waiting for a bus or train. It showed newsreels, cartoons and short features.

Opposite: BRIGHTON HIPPODROME, *c.* 1909. This was the town's main variety theatre at this time, attracting many famous acts. It was extended in 1939, and a number of important plays were staged there, but it is no longer a theatre.

WEST STREET AND ODEON CINEMA, *c.* 1946. The Odeon is overshadowed in this picture by the tower of St Paul's church, with its octagonal lantern spire (built in 1846/8). The super-cinema was opened in December 1937, and closed in 1973, when it was replaced by the Kingswest Odeon.

THE SCALA CINEMA, *c.* 1930s. This was in Western Road and had a succession of name changes since it was built in 1909. At the time this photograph was taken, it had a pit orchestra and was showing a mixture of new talkies and silent films, having previously advertised 'No talkies here'.

94

BRIGHTON RACE COURSE, 1790. A print of the race course not long after the first races in 1783. In 1784, the Prince of Wales visited the course, and this helped to make it popular. The first stand was built in 1788.

BRIGHTON RACE COURSE, early 1900s. The corporation took over the course in 1888 and the stand was used as an ammunition store in the First World War. Early in its history, the race course was threatened with being ploughed up by an irate farmer, who claimed that he was owed money by the Jockey Club. As soon as his ploughman started operations, 'the press gang' put in an appearance, and the farm workers rapidly disappeared.

BRIGHTON CARNIVAL, 1927. These were some of the collectors hoping to extract coins from the public in aid of the hospital on 4 June 1927. The carnival was held annually from about 1922, replacing earlier similar celebrations, such as the St Bartholomew's Day Fair on the cliff top, and later The Level.

CROWD AT BRIGHTON AND HOVE ALBION MATCH, 1920s. The first professional football team was Brighton United (1798/1900). The Brighton and Hove Rangers team was also formed at that time and in 1902 changed its name to the Brighton and Hove Albion. (The name 'Wiles' displayed in the photograph was the photographer who produced the postcard.)

THE STAFF AT THE GOLDSTONE FOOTBALL GROUND, HOVE, 1919/20. The Albion team played at the County Cricket Ground in 1901/2, and later moved to the Goldstone Ground, which previously formed part of Goldstone Farm. The greatest day in the club's history was 21 May 1983, when they drew 2-2 with Manchester United in the FA Cup at Wembley, before 100,000 spectators.

EAST HOVE FOOTBALL CLUB, 1910/11. A proud team of young players from Hove. From the nineteenth century onwards football has been a very popular sport in the Brighton area with many amateur and school teams flourishing.

SUSSEX v SURREY CRICKET SPECTATORS, HOVE, 1911. We first hear of a Brighton cricket team in 1754 and the first Brighton club was formed in 1791. The game was played on The Old Steine until it was banned by the town's Master of Ceremonies in 1787. The present-day club was established in 1839 and moved to the County Ground in 1872.

SUSSEX COUNTY CRICKET TEAM AT BRIGHTON, 1930. In this year A.H.H. Gilligan was Captain, and the team held seventh position in the Championship. There have been good cricket players in Brighton for a long time. A story is told of the Duke of Queensberry, who could not resist a wager. When staying at Brighton in the eighteenth century, he was challenged to convey a letter fifty miles in an hour. He enclosed it in a cricket ball, which was thrown from one player to another in a long line. The feat was accomplished in less than the hour.

CHILDREN AND MAYPOLE, *c.* 1911. This was at St Michael's school, Portslade. The Maypole was of the ribbon plaiting variety, introduced to England from Europe in the nineteenth century. Although not traditionally English, it soon became very popular in schools and remains so to the present day.

SKIPPING AT BRIGHTON FISH MARKET, GOOD FRIDAY, *c.* 1936. The Good Friday custom of skipping survived longer at Brighton than at many other places, especially among the fishermen and their families. In fact, Good Friday was often referred to as 'Long Rope Day'. The ropes used for skipping were those used by the fishermen in their daily work and were said to be symbolic of the rope used by Judas to hang himself. Skipping at Brighton also went on at The Level. It died out during the Second World War but now and then meets with a revival.

THE BATMAN OF BRIGHTON, GOOD FRIDAY, *c.* 1938. This picture shows the traditional game of 'Bat and Trap' (also known as 'Trap Bat' or 'Bat and Ball') which has been associated with Good Friday and Brighton for longer than anyone can remember. The teams who played on The Level were usually organised by local pubs or the Brighton Labour Club. At one time the losing team had to buy a barrel of beer.

BAT AND TRAP ON THE LEVEL, GOOD FRIDAY, *c.* 1938. The game, long popular in Brighton and other places in Sussex, also had its counterparts in other counties where it was known by a variety of names such as Piggy, Cattie, and Buck and Stick. There is a close similarity to the ancient games of Tip-Cat and Knur-and-Spel. Bat and Trap on The Level was remembered as a glorious romp but now the tradition has lapsed and many Bat and Trap sets have ended up in museums.

Six
People and Personalities

GYPSIES AT PYCOMBE. A typical gypsy family halted on the roadside verge in April 1938. Although horse-owning gypsies were diminishing there were still scenes such as this to be seen around Brighton before the Second World War.

NINETEENTH CENTURY FAMILY GROUP. Studio photographers such as this one were at the peak of their popularity in the late nineteenth century. The family group is un-named, and papa appears to be missing. The family were photographed by Mr G. Cassinello, in his studio at 60 Middle Street, Brighton. He advertised himself as 'Miniature Painter, Portrait and Landscape Photographer' and was in business at this address from 1867 to 1874, then he moved to 44 Ship Street until 1880.

TWO NINETEENTH-CENTURY DANDIES. The photographer was Mr William Hall of 80 West Street, Brighton. He was there from 1875 to 1897 having previously been at St James Street, North Street, and on the West Pier. From 1891 he was joined in business by his son. Unfortunately, we do not know the names of these two well-dressed young men.

TWO LADIES AND CHILD. A slightly later studio photograph, probably early 1900s, from Donovan's Studios at 1c St James Street, where he was in business from 1879. The ladies' hats are very spectacular and typical of the period. Note the pseudo woodland background provided by the photographer.

FUNERAL OF DEAR LITTLE ANNIE ROBINSON, 29 July 1909. The caption on this card reads, 'Crowds at the graveside'. There were many children there, which is very typical of funerals in this period. The sender of the card has made certain that the recipient spots two of her friends among those present by marking them with 'X' and 'O'. Apparently, the actual sender of the card was not there.

FUNERAL OF CAPTAIN FRED COLLINS, 4 September 1912. Captain Collins was a local Brighton celebrity and skipper of the *Skylark* pleasure boats. Attending the funeral were ten of his crew, plus a great many townsfolk. The date given on this card appears to be wrong by a month.

FUNERAL OF CAPTAIN COLLINS, 4 September 1912. Captain Collins was a familiar figure on the seafront, having spent sixty years around the beach as a lifeboatman, and owner of the *Skylark* boats. He was noted for always wearing a dark straw boater hat. This postcard is by a different photographer, who has got his date right.

FREDERICK EVERSHED (1826-1899). This fine old gentleman moved from Seaford to Brighton in the mid-nineteenth century, becoming a tallow chandler in Lower College Street. His sons followed him into the trade and in 1903 they advertised themselves as 'Sperm and paraffin wax candle makers, soap manufacturers, and makers of the celebrated Dolphin paraffin soap'. Their works were at Eastern Road and Foundry Street. The business eventually moved to Shoreham, where they became wholesale grocers.

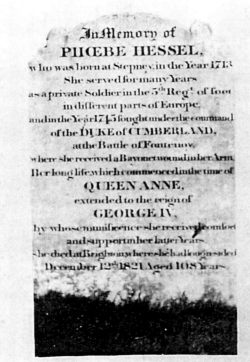

In Memory of
PHŒBE HESSEL,
who was born at Stepney, in the Year 1713.
She served for many Years
as a private Soldier in the 5th Reg.t of foot
in different parts of Europe,
and in the Year 1745 fought under the command
of the DUKE of CUMBERLAND,
at the Battle of Fontenoy,
where she received a Bayonet wound in her Arm.
Her long life, which commenced in the time of
QUEEN ANNE,
extended to the reign of
GEORGE IV,
by whose munificence she received comfort
and support in her later Years.
She died at Brighton, where she had long resided
December 12th 1821 Aged 108 Years.

THE GRAVESTONE OF PHOEBE HESSEL IN ST NICHOLAS'S CHURCHYARD. Phoebe Hessel was born at Stepney in 1713, and died at Brighton in 1821, aged 108. The gravestone gives the history of this unusual lady who served as a male soldier in the army and in 1745 fought under the Duke of Cumberland at the Battle of Fontinoy, where she was wounded. She became a local celebrity, the Prince Regent calling her 'A jolly old fellow' and awarding her a pension. However, it has to be said that posterity has cast a few doubts on some of her claims to fame.

MARTHA GUNN.

MARTHA GUNN, 1727-1815. Brighton's most famous 'Dipper' or bathing woman. She was a favourite of the Prince Regent and in her day became very much a local celebrity. At her funeral, forty of her friends followed in the procession. See also page 13.

WOUNDED FROM THE PAVILION HOSPITAL, FIRST WORLD WAR. The Royal Pavilion was used as a military hospital during most of the war. The Indians were there until 1916, and from 1916 to 1919 it was used as a hospital for limbless men, with 6,085 admissions in total. These were just six of them, looking remarkably happy in the circumstances.

Seven

Trams, Trains and Other Transport

LONDON, BRIGHTON AND SOUTH COAST RAILWAY DELIVERY CART, early 1900s. The coming of the railway to Brighton and other parts of the South Coast not only revolutionised travel for locals and visitors, it also made it much cheaper and easier to send even heavy and large goods and packages from one place to another – even remote villages. The railway had its own system of delivery from station to destination, by means of horse drawn carts such as this, which continued with little change until after the Second World War.

'THE SKYLARK', 1905. There was not just one 'Skylark' pleasure boat, but at least three, the first being in use from 1852. Captain Fred Collins, the skipper, was said to have coined the immortal phrase, 'Any more for the Skylark'. In the late nineteenth-century, a one hour trip cost just one shilling.

The "SKYLARK" ready to leave BRIGHTON.

'THE SKYLARK', early 1900s. A more romanticised view of the *Skylark* setting out from Brighton beach, with a group of would-be passengers adding interest to the picture. Daisy Noakes in *The Town Beehive* (written in the 1970s), recalled one of the *Skylark* boats which was motorised and made trips between the piers. A concertina player provided a rendition of *Over the Waves* the day she rode in the boat. Two of Captain Collins' *Skylarks* took part in the Dunkirk evacuation and were lost.

GOING FOR A SAIL AT BRIGHTON, early 1900s. This is clearly Brighton beach, with the familiar Pier outline, one of the distinctive beach seats and even an attractive old bath-chair. But the boat looks a little strange and the whole picture has an odd, crowded, air about it. Perhaps the postcard manufacturer decided to embellish his picture with a few extra details.

'THE BRIGHTON QUEEN', early 1900s. One of Brighton's paddle-steamers close to The West Pier. This was the first of the two Queens, built in 1897 and used by the Navy in the Second World War. A second *Brighton Queen* was sunk in 1940 when assisting in the Dunkirk evacuation.

THE 'GLEN ROSA' PADDLE-STEAMER, early 1900s. This was the twin of *The Brighton Queen*, shown close to the West Pier. The pier was a popular call for steamers making trips to places along the coast, or even as far as The Isle of Wight.

BOATS NEAR THE WEST PIER, *c.* 1911. This has long been a familiar sight. Brighton fishermen once used their own special kind of boats, known as 'Hogboats' or 'Hoggies', which were particularly suited to local conditions. Some were ultimately sawn in half and used as primitive homes. The very last of the 'Hoggies' was reputedly burnt on Bonfire Night in the 1880s, a night always very popular with the Brighton fishermen.

BRIGHTON PLEASURE STEAMER, late nineteenth or early twentieth-century. Although I cannot closely identify this picture, it seemed too good to omit. The passengers seem to be almost entirely men, so perhaps it was a trip commissioned by a male organisation.

BIPLANE OVER WEST PIER, *c.* 1913. This was perhaps not entirely a novelty for Brighton folk at this time, as planes had been flying to the town from 1910 and there was even an air race from London to Brighton in 1913. In 1911, a plane flew from Brookland Aerodrome, near Weybridge, in one hour, the prop later hung in the Royal York Hotel as a souvenir.

PLANE ON THE SEA AT BRIGHTON, early 1900s. A sea-plane station was opened at Brighton in 1913 by Magnus Volk's son, Herman, at Banjo Groyne, using the Volk's electric railway for access. The hanger was requisitioned for the war in 1914.

'GRAF ZEPPELIN' OVER THE PALACE PIER. An aeroship flew over Brighton in 1910, but this picture must be later than that. All is not what it seems, however. The airship has almost certainly been added to a fairly ordinary photograph of the Pier, in order to stimulate sales. Even the quantity of sailing boats look a little suspect. The picture postcard bears the inscription on the reverse side, 'This is a real photograph!'

LONDON GENERAL OMNIBUS AT VICTORIA GARDENS, BRIGHTON 1935. This was Silver Jubilee year, and, as there are signs of patriotic decorations on an upper balcony, we can assume that this bus, which is far away from its normal route, was taking part in local celebrations.

VANGUARD MOTOR BUS ACCIDENT, 12 July 1906. The Vanguard bus was on its way to Brighton with a group of firemen on a day trip from Kent. As it speeded down a hill towards Brighton, the brakes failed, and the bus crashed into a tree. Ten of the occupants were killed or wounded, making headlines in the newspapers the next day. The first regular London to Brighton motor coach was a Vanguard which ran from 1905.

OLD SHIP HOTEL AND CARS, 1908. In 1906, The Old Ship became the headquarters of the Automobile Club and the cars in this picture are taking part in a motor rally. The iron lamp standards were removed in 1909 after one had been damaged by a car. The hotel's attractive window blinds were fitted in 1890, at a cost of just over £133.

THE OLD BERKELEY STAGE COACH. This was one of the Brighton to London coaches which called at The Old Ship Hotel. Later it was taken to the USA. The Golden Age of coaching was from 1820 until the coming of the railways in 1841. By 1843 only one coach was still operating, attracting just old-fashioned and timid passengers. In 1862 a revival began (something like the preserved steam railways today) with enthusiasts running coaches as a nostalgic adventure. The last coach to run regularly from Brighton ('The Vigilant') was in 1905, and the First World War completely killed the revival.

THE VANDERBILT COACH AT BRIGHTON, early 1900s. The coach, *Nimrod*, was claimed to be the fastest on the road during the coach revival. Alfred Gwynne Vanderbilt was a romantic gentleman and famous horseman. He lost his life in 1915 in the sinking of the great liner, the *Lusitania*.

THE VANDERBILT COACH PASSING THE OLD SHIP HOTEL, early 1900s. The cyclists in this picture are obviously struggling to keep up with the coach for as long as possible.

THE FIRST JOURNEY OF THE VANDERBILT COACH TO BRIGHTON, 22 April 1908.
Mr Vanderbilt said that the proudest day of his life was when he drove his coach on this
journey.

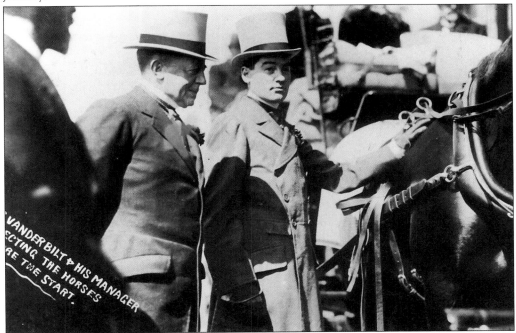

MR VANDERBILT AND HIS MANAGER INSPECTING THE HORSES. This was outside
the Metropole Hotel, Brighton, during the 1911 coaching season; towards the end of the short-
lived revival. The impeccable dress of the two men was typical of the romantic image which was
being created.

MR VANDERBILT'S COACH AT DALE HILL, NEAR BRIGHTON, c. 1908. This was during the romantic revival of the early twentieth-century. During the earlier golden age of coaching, 28 coaches ran daily from London to Brighton, taking 6 hours. Later, the number increased to 52, and in one year 15 horses died following continuous galloping in order to beat rivals.

THE BRIGHTON HORSE SHOW, 1907. When horses were the kings of the road, local business firms were justly proud of their turnouts. These were shown off annually at local horse shows such as this one, attracting large crowds.

EMPTY BEER KEGS RETURNING TO BRIGHTON, early 1900s. A steam lorry used by the Rock Brewery, on its way back to its home base, possibly in St James Street. The brewery, one of many in Brighton, was established around 1809, and continued in business until 1928.

TOLL-HOUSE ON THE LEWES-BRIGHTON ROAD, late nineteenth century. From 1770, the Lewes to Brighton road was maintained by a turnpike trust, with toll-gates at the Bear Inn and at Kingston. Although the tolls helped to improve Sussex roads, they were always very unpopular and many ruses were adopted to avoid payment.

TANDEM ON BRIGHTON SEAFRONT, early 1900s. Was this the original bicycle made for two in Harry Dacre's popular *Daisy, Daisy* song? It is perhaps more likely to be the tandem made by the Sussex inventor James Starley in the village of Albourne on which the couple sat side by side.

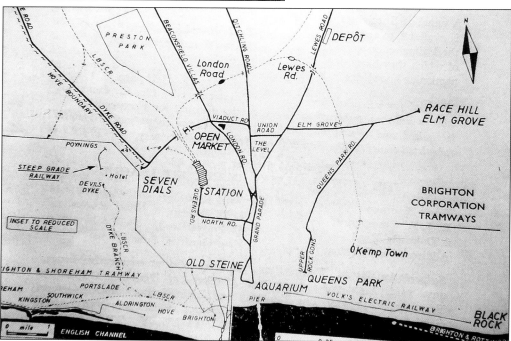

BRIGHTON TRAM MAP, *c.* 1901. Trams were once an important part of the Brighton traffic scene and here is a map of their routes. At branch lines, there was a points boy to operate the switches. Although only about fourteen years old, he wore a tramways uniform. When technology took over, the points were operated electrically.

HOVE TO SHOREHAM HORSE DRAWN TRAM, late nineteenth century. This tram line was opened by the Brighton and District Tramways Company. Steam traction was used at first and then horses. This photograph shows the Shoreham end of the line, near the railway station.

BRIGHTON CORPORATION TRAM, early 1900s. The trams ran in the town from 1901, initially charging one penny fare for any distance. A typical journey time was eight minutes from the railway station to the Steine. The last trams ran in Brighton in 1939.

Barbarous Murder

In a Railway Carriage,

NEAR BRIGHTON.

A fearful murder has been committed on the London and Brighton Railway, an old gentleman named Gold having been stabbed in many places, and thrown from the carriage on to the line, where he was found dead. The police are in search of the murderer.

Tune—Just before the Battle Mother.

A fearful crime we are revealing,
　Committed on a Railway line,
Murder there is no concealing,
　It always leave some fearful sign,
On the London and Brighton Railway,
　A wealthy gentleman named Gold,
In the open light of noon day,
　For his money his life was sold.

In the open light of noon day,
　Cover'd with blood and dead and cold,
Upon the London and Brighton Railway,
　They found the body of Mr. Gold.

His London business he transacted,
　And was returning home again,
Then the crime was enacted,
　That we must tell with grief and pain,
In a first-class carriage he was riding,
　He'll travel on that line no more,
A ruffian must have sat beside him,
　And laid him lifeless in his gore.

On the line, alas, they found him,
　His poor old face by wounds were torn,
Streams of blood lay around him,
　His watch and money, and life was gone.
Another man who travell'd with him,
　Said he saw the fatal strife,
Some countryman had killed the victim,
　And also tried to take my life.

The man who gave the information,
　To be much hurt he did pretend,
The police without much hesitation,
　To his home Lefroy did send ;
The policemen at the front door waited,
　It was bad judgement we must say,
To lose their prisoner they were fated,
　Lefroy escaped by the back way.

The victim sold his life so dearly,
　The blood upon the carriage shows,
His many wounds tell us clearly,
　Of nearly twenty deadly blows ;
From his face the blood was streaming,
　Of a deadly struggle every sign,
While the summer sun was beaming,
　His body was thrown upon the line.

We hope this crime they will unavel,
　And the murderer bring to light,
It is hardly safe to travel,
　Either by day or by night.
Mr. Gold has fell a victim,
　The murderer must no longer fly,
If a jury shall convict him,
　I'm sure you'll say he ought to die.

London :—H. SUCH, Machine Printer, & Publisher, 177, Union-street, Boro'. S. E.

MURDER ON THE BRIGHTON LINE, 27 JUNE 1881. A street broadsheet produced after the murder of Frederick Gold by Arthur Lefroy, on a train from London to Brighton. After the killing, Lefroy opened the carriage door and pushed the old man onto the tracks. The murderer was arrested at Brighton and subsequently convicted and hanged. This broadsheet was typical of such productions which were printed and sold to the crowds attending the criminal's execution.

BRIGHTON RAILWAY STATION AND QUEENS ROAD, early 1900s. It took 3,500 men and over 500 horses to build the station. Rail fares from London in the early part of this century were relatively cheap and the crowds that flocked to Brighton and other South Coast towns, completely changed their appearance from sleepy seaside havens to open air amusement parks. In this busy picture, the tram vies for custom with the horse-drawn bus.

INTERIOR OF BRIGHTON STATION, late nineteenth-century. The station was built on an artificial plateau cut out of the Dyke Road ridge. A chalk cliff may be seen on the western side of the station. The building was designed by David Mocatta (1806-82), who was the architect behind many of the stations on the London, Brighton, and South Coast Railway.

BRIGHTON STATION. An undated picture of a visitor to Brighton station, the L & NWR locomotive *Titan*. The London to Brighton line was opened in 1841, and soon Brighton gained a further title to add to all its others : 'London by the Sea'. During the first ten years of the line, 3,000 new houses were built in Brighton. In 1860 a music-hall song promised, 'The excursion train to Brighton, at a cost of half-a-crown'.

KEMP TOWN STATION, 1900. A branch to Kemp Town was opened in 1869. This was a short line (under 2 miles), but it required a 50 ft high viaduct across the Lewes Road and a tunnel 1,000 yards long. It was the motor bus which finally killed off the line in 1932.

CLAYTON TUNNEL ON THE BRIGHTON LINE, *c.* 1918. The tunnel was one of the great Victorian engineering feats – 2,259 yards long, and originally lit by gas along the whole length, 'to induce a feeling of confidence and cheerfulness among the passengers' as they neared Brighton. The castle-like structure on the southern end of the tunnel was also said to give the public a feeling of security although the railwayman's cottage on the top was a bit of a let-down.

VOLK'S ELECTRIC RAILWAY, early 1900s. From 1883, visitors to Brighton could enjoy a ride on the country's first electric railway. It had been built by Magnus Volk, the son of a German clockmaker, who had married a Sussex girl and settled in Brighton. The rail line was originally about a quarter of a mile long, but it was so popular that Magnus was given permission to extend it. In the first six months of 1884, 200,000 passengers travelled on it.

THE TERMINUS OF VOLK'S RAILWAY AT BLACK ROCK, 1912. There are many pictures of Volk's railway, but few show the end of the line at Black Rock (possibly because the surroundings were rather bleak and not very photogenic). The message on the reverse of the postcard says, 'The cars take about ten minutes to do the journey. The stations are rather like F's toy ones'. The card was sent from Brighton to Eastbourne on 25 January 1913.

VOLK'S RAILWAY AND A ROUGH SEA. This picture is dated 1916, and shows how the little electric railway had to confront the elements on many occasions.

'DADDY LONG LEGS' OR 'THE SPIDER', early 1900s. This was Magnus Volk's attempt at something rather more imaginative than his original railway. It ran for three miles along the sea bed to Rottingdean, the passengers being carried in a saloon with iron legs. The whole thing ran on rails fixed in concrete under the water. The children play below, completely unperturbed by the strange monster towering over them.

CHILDREN IN GOAT CART, *c.* 1918. These little carts were popular with children in Brighton and other South Coast seaside towns. They were perhaps less popular with adults, and certainly with the authorities, who tended to dismiss them as messy and smelly.

TWO ON A DONKEY ON BRIGHTON BEACH, *c.* 1910. Our final picture, and although rather suspect in the way the subjects appear, it is typical of the joy and innocence of pre-First World War days at Brighton. After that, things were never quite the same.